# THE OYSTERS
# I BRING TO
# BANQUETS

*Essential Poets Series 296*

 **Canada Council** **Conseil des Arts**
**for the Arts** **du Canada**

**ONTARIO ARTS COUNCIL**
**CONSEIL DES ARTS DE L'ONTARIO**
an Ontario government agency
un organisme du gouvernement de l'Ontario

Guernica Editions Inc. acknowledges the support of the Canada Council
for the Arts and the Ontario Arts Council. The Ontario Arts Council
is an agency of the Government of Ontario.

We acknowledge the financial support of the Government of Canada.

# THE OYSTERS I BRING TO BANQUETS

*Gary Geddes*

**GUERNICA
EDITIONS**
TORONTO · CHICAGO · BUFFALO · LANCASTER (U.K.)
2022

Guernica Founder: Antonio D'Alfonso

Michael Mirolla, editor
David Moratto, cover and interior design
Front cover image: A detail from "The Feast of the Gods 1514/1529,"
by Giovanni Bellini and Titian. Author photo by Ann Eriksson.
Guernica Editions Inc.
287 Templemead Drive, Hamilton (ON), Canada L8W 2W4
2250 Military Road, Tonawanda, N.Y. 14150-6000 U.S.A.
www.guernicaeditions.com

Distributors:
Independent Publishers Group (IPG)
600 North Pulaski Road, Chicago IL 60624
University of Toronto Press Distribution (UTP)
5201 Dufferin Street, Toronto (ON), Canada M3H 5T8
Gazelle Book Services
White Cross Mills, High Town, Lancaster LA1 4XS U.K.

First edition.
Printed in Canada.

Legal Deposit—Third Quarter
Library of Congress Catalog Card Number: 2021950131
Library and Archives Canada Cataloguing in Publication
Title: The oysters I bring to banquets / Gary Geddes.
Names: Geddes, Gary, 1940- author.
Series: Essential poets ; 296.
Description: First edition. | Series statement: Essential poets series ; 296 | Poems.
Identifiers: Canadiana 2021036873X | ISBN 9781771837101 (softcover)
Classification: LCC PS8563.E3 O97 2022 | DDC C811/.54—dc23

*The power of sound has always been greater than the power of sense.*

—JOSEPH CONRAD

# Contents

## Termites

# The Greenhouse Effect

# Family Matters

## *Peripatetic*

# Termites

*Art is our chief means of
breaking bread with the dead.*

—W.H. Auden

# Elegy

*for John Asfour*

Lebanon, a curious
boy, a shiny object in the sand
outside his village. With

all the lights switched
off and small metal particles
removed from his eyes,

his ruined optic nerves,
he explodes into poetry. Words
that have limped along,

taking no responsibility for themselves,
shape up and begin, slowly, to bear
weight, acquire beauty,

raise smiles,
like the one that spreads
across faces in East Jerusalem

as children in the orphanage
cling to his arms and legs,
John bent over the *oud,*

singing old familiar tunes in Arabic.
As for the loss, he makes
light of it, laughter

his tonic of choice unless,
of course, it is 'love,' a concept
dismissed as sentimental

but worn like a diminutive heart
or cryptic hieroglyph on the sleeve.
A joke or satirical comment

on Israeli-Palestinian relations, beaming
faces dappled by sunlight filtered
through grape-vines overhead.

Obliged to talk politics: Bedouins
displaced again in the Negev, Saeb Erekat,
a walk near Abraham's well.

Propped up in palliative care and flirting
with the duty nurse, he winces as the needle
releases a surge of morphine

into his vein. The new drug promised
reprieve, shrunk the tumour in his lung
to half its size, then stopped,

outflanked by fully-armed sleeper
cells. The dark archive of his poems
never raises the question why,

the flight of birds, a line of golden
wheat against the blue
of sky.

# Captive Audience

Five months in jail and still no answer,
faithful Muusa not returned, desert
sands rife with renegades. Fighter jets

bomb Hargeisa, the Sheik's harem
defect one by one. Unclaimed bodies
rot in the streets. How do sophisticated

cultures end like this? It starts with
small gifts, the impossibility of
not favouring your own. Next,

the struggle over sequestered aid,
donor labels still intact, followed by
the pecking order: Ruler of Toilet Rolls,

Vizier of Canned Veggies, Excellency
of Powdered Eggs, fat cats always greediest.
The prison grapevine serves us well

as a conduit for news and gossip,
revives then kills the spirit, hope its
latest casualty. We had a Buddhist Brit

in the same cell-block, picked up
for selling drugs. His problem?
Dealing with the wrong people.

He went on about Noble Truths:
suffering caused by desire, reprieve
found in right speech and right living.

When word got out he was trying
to convert us good Muslims, they fed
his tongue to dogs. News from Ogaden

as might be expected: Siad Barre's tanks
explode like over-stimulated Coke
bottles. We're better off with camels

and rifles than the crazy potpourri
of imported ordnance. Poetry
is more persuasive than combat,

Hadraawi argued, as infectious
as bagpipes and less painful
on the ears. Nonetheless, it too

landed him in jail. Rally the tropes,
supercharge the metaphors, let them
gather force, strike home, seduce

and overwhelm the opposition,
unorthodox as termite mounds,
so easily mistaken for the enemy.

# All That Rain

Once I had a voice, K says, watching foam
settle in his glass of beer, but I never learned
to play an instrument. Too much death,

bad luck and a peripatetic father. I recall
sitting at a concert in the community
centre where this woman with fractious

brown hair was introduced and began
to play the violin. I focussed on Natasha,
imbibed her repertoire of songs, from movies

thought forgotten. A reservoir of memories,
feelings long buried. And all that rain.
*Umbrellas of Cherbourg. Moon River.* And

that day in Grade 12 French when Charles
Trenet's rendition of "La Mer" made me weep.
Natasha had strewn leaves on the floor,

autumn leaves among vegetables, a bottle
of red wine, harvest bounty to simulate
a time and place where the making of music

seemed natural, necessary. My foot tapping
the beat, I hummed, fighting back the impulse
to sing along. If only I could make words

dance, I thought, drawn across an auditory
nerve of vibrating catgut, verbal fingering
so deft they'd leap an octave or two, achieve

the change of register that makes a listener
gasp, seductive minor chords that fly beneath
the radar, nest in the ear, a passionate

repertoire of pure sound. I recalled a young
Catherine Deneuve as Genevieve, with Guy,
Madelaine and Fate, their simple narrative

of love and loss, actors struggling to hint
at what the heartstrings yearn to convey. Guy,
returned too late from the war in Algeria,

found his beloved already married. He operates
a small gas station in Cherbourg now. From
the expensive car idling at the pumps,

Genevieve walks in, shakes her umbrella,
flashes a smile of recognition and asks
how he is. Guy, tiny son perched on a stool

behind the till, sums up a life of wounds,
disappointments, with *je vais bien*, I'm fine.
By the time Natasha finished her medley

of tunes, I'd melted and did not know what
to say, but I could feel that warm rain, its
insistent patter, drumming inside my skull.

K's right index finger traces a path through
the condensation on his untouched glass.
He looks up at me, smiling, and shrugs.

# J-35

Do animals cry? she asks.
I don't know, I say, but I think

they grieve. I'd read about a camel
that sniffed her dead offspring

for days and wouldn't move
until they placed its pelt on her

back. Why do you ask? Her hand
on the breakfast counter looks tiny

beside mine. A milk–ring graces
her mouth, a toasted bread-crumb

clings to her cheek. A sympathetic
smile is all I have to offer.

J-35, she says, scarcely audible.
The orca in the news has carried

her dead calf for fourteen days,
trying to keep it above water,

travelling hundreds of miles
as J-pod forages for the scarce

spring salmon. When it isn't
resting on her head she grips

its tail with her teeth. J-35 knows
her baby's dead, she whispers;

I think she's trying to tell us
something. I leave the science

out for now: the most polluted
mammals on earth, the slurry

of toxins female orcas slough off
on their newborns. Extinction

looming, salmon stocks
depleted. Tanker traffic, the

old whale-road the Vikings
celebrated now a web of dirty

shipping lanes, booming
grounds, plastic archipelagos.

I think you're right, I say,
let's see what we can do.

# *Hiatus*

Delicate snowflakes settle on the tidal
flat, whose reflective surface turns

from forest-green to gunmetal grey.
Outside my window a hummingbird,

wings a blur, dips its long, elegant beak
into the fluted glass tube of the feeder.

Nearby, jays and towhees vie for access
to the hanging cylinder of black-oil

sunflower seeds, a chestnut-backed
chickadee and a purple finch assess

their chance to chow. Beyond snow-laden
moorage rafts, sheets of frozen water

form in the shallows. Only burning wood
and humming fridge disturb the silence.

# Disaster Management

One question dogs her still, despite
credentials: why this particular
child? A job, a foreign assignment,

the chance to use skills acquired
in the Emergency and Disaster Relief
program, patrolling beaches, binoculars

in hand, feet raw and sweating in cheap
gumboots, emails from family, concerned
friends. Phone at the ready, she'll adjust

the lens for distance and focus, hoping
to spot derelict vessels, inflatable dinghies
in time to save lives, but wishing too

for empty horizons swept only by
foraging gulls. Nothing in the web-based
learning materials and occasional lectures

has prepared her for this, not even
the chapter called Dealing With Disaster.
Both instructors warned of panic,

hunger, hypothermia, but not death,
perhaps because the dead, lying there,
passage paid, journey ended, require

neither haste nor care. But what
of this graduate, her degree or diploma
in the mail, expected to roll with perils,

unforeseen punches, including that small
boy facedown on the beach, his family
denied admission as refugees,

lying palms up, as if asleep, water
lapping his forehead. It's the red t-shirt,
and orange rubber soles that stay

with her back home, jogging the waterfront
path around Stanley Park, passengers
waving at her from a passing cruise ship.

# *Grooming*

Me? I've no passion for horse racing,
although I love the soft velvety flesh
around their muzzles. It seems those parts
had been designed not just for grazing

but for nuzzling. I cringe at the way bits
cut into mouths and riding crops leave welts
that take days to heal. So there's no chance
you'll catch me weighing the odds and placing

bets. I'm more likely be found hanging out
in stables comforting the losers, horse
*and* jockey. One of my favourites dropped
dead just past the clubhouse turn, injuring

the thrown rider who died in hospital
later, both having overtaxed their hearts,
driven themselves quite literally into
the ground, not the expected finish-line.

A well-shod animal has the best chance
of completing a race without damage.
Once, inspecting the hooves, I detected
a nail missing in the light aluminum

shoe, a sure sign of negligence, perhaps
a wilful dereliction, the left front
hoof where the concussive force is strongest
and shoddy workmanship most likely to

take its toll. What was a mere groom to do,
report the omission to the owner,
confront the farrier, when one or both
could be complicit, clued in, on the make?

My duty like that of a bridegroom
was to the central figure in the drama,
whose elegance and spirit we extol,
even though it cost me my job, my joy.

# April 2020

One day this will all be history,
she says. A dubious consolation,
he thought, so will we. Statistics

or brief footnotes about the one
who survived with a ventilator
made of garden hose? Marginalia

added later by a monkish scribe
struggling with the last remaining
computer, just long enough

to embellish the capital letters
of your name, unless that name
is e.e. cummings. Shops shut, ferry

service shortened or cancelled,
the few exceptions charged with
strict rules and passenger limits,

exorbitant fines for exhaling
in public, washrooms verboten,
toilet paper pilfered. How

rapidly we've morphed
from celebrating the global
village and its alleged solidarity

Gary Geddes

to giving neighbours and friends
a dirty look or closed fist if they get
too chummy in the check-out queue.

The birds, at least, are striking up
a tune, putting the finishing touches
on their nests and courtship rituals.

# Light Housekeeping

*for Marilynn Robinson*


Downward dip as the train slips from bridge trestle
into the slick, black waters of the lake,
where hearts wrestle

with loss, brains reel, mortar and pestle, images
of grandfather, ticket punch in hand,
flailing about, pages

adrift as windows burst
inward and the deep engulfs late-night
gamblers, thirsts

quenched at last, ages
irrelevant now and the dealt hand, doomed
sleepers awake to the instant

of their release, the reverse
umbilicus, metal aslant delivering them
womb-ward, offering little refuge

in the flight from air,
time, perhaps, to observe a stuffed
woolly bear

hurtle past, making a beeline
for the surface, a reminder
bobbing in black ink, message

duly noted, tucked into a binder
and mother, shortly after, her trajectory
lakeward, the car turning

twice in mid-air, and the rectory
kitchen abuzz, the link
obvious, heads nodding, tea

served, white bread (no crust),
jam, a trace of polite repartee
from those who know survival

a game of chance, every face
pale, thinking fish, blue lips,
the limits of grace.

# Pickwick's Papers

As layers of paper multiply
on his desk, the sense of chaos
mounts. Pens and flash-drives
disappear, paper clips, unpaid

bills migrate out of sight.
Nothing a strong wind or well
placed wooden match won't cure.
The daybook or Handy Pocket

Minder from Home Hardware
with last year's dates, repository
of things not done, appointments
missed. A trinity of burnt-out

light bulbs, spiral notebooks
started but discontinued as less
and less seems worth recording.
Plastic pill bottles, all empty,

line the shelf of unread books,
foreign languages languish
in dusty dictionaries, forgotten
photos bide their time in neglected

albums. Volumes nine and ten
of the *OED*, their inordinate number
of words beginning with the letter
'S,' recall the vanishing verbs

and negligent nouns refusing
to appear when summoned,
only to wander nonchalantly
across the neo-cortex when no

longer needed. A squat Victorian
ceramic vase, with a pink-cheeked
figure painted on one side, blue
waistcoat, plaid vest, a jackknife

and half a dozen ballpoint pens
protruding from his hollow skull,
Peter's surprise gift just months
after his retirement as a London

publisher, divesting treasures, one
at a time, not a book, but a character
from one of Dickens' novels. Beside
Mr. Pickwick, you'll find a slim volume

of love letters between Olga Knipper
and Anton Chekhov turned into a play
called *I take your hand in mine*, half buried
between printer and silent black phone.

# Matins

He rises early, turns on the radio.
As water heats up in the tea kettle,
he learns of further unmarked graves

discovered at a former residential
school, a huge troop build-up
at Russia's border with Ukraine,

more Saudi air-strikes on rebel forces
in Yemen, a million Uyghurs facing
involuntary re-education in Xinjiang,

Palestinians planting olive trees attacked
by settlers armed with clubs, ocean
levels rising, heat domes, atmospheric

rivers,  a child struck by a distracted
driver, viral lockdowns, hospitals
overwhelmed. A red light indicates

the water has boiled. As the teabag
bleeds in the brimming blue mug, he can
feel the termites gnawing at his timbers.

## Coming to Your Senses

Focus on small things,
enough to take your mind
off what you cannot

have. Or can't afford.
On the forest walk you're
taking, does the bright green

of ferns against the rusty
orange of fallen leaves
re-charge your storage

cells? Do you quietly
take stock of the riches
in angled, forgiving light,

fir and cedar branches
clothed in moss and lichen,
all emerald and dripping?

And underfoot, that tiny
cluster of mushrooms,
their beaming faces taking

refuge beneath a leaf, proof
of the vigorous production
of nutrients, the passing on

of information, roots
of the leaning arbutus
whispering to the maple

that the antiquated geezer
on the path mimics the moss
we know as old man's beard?

So much for science and
visual stimuli. What about
the sharp sweet smell

of pine, the resins and terpenes
conifers release? With such
abundance, such sensory over-

load, you just might have to save
the operatic exuberance
of bird-song for another time.

## Etched in the Flesh

Who's this? It's you, I say, pressing a forefinger
gently on your collarbone just above the pale rim
of blue hospital gown. You hold the photo

with both hands about ten inches from your face.
At 96, your eyes and sagging muscles strain
to grasp this youthful version of yourself,

lovely, seventeen, skin smooth as marble,
the original black & white colour-enhanced.
Minutes pass. I'd love to know what's going on

as you ponder this dazzling enigma. I've been
singing, holding your hand, trying to recreate
in words a few shared moments you might remember.

After the third stanza of Beautiful Dreamer
you squeeze my hand and say: You're quite
the charmer. Are you complimenting a stepson

doing his damnedest to delay the inevitable
or trying to cool off a potential suitor?
That's when I recall a story you once told me

of the French foreman at the munitions
factory in Scarborough, who wanted
to sleep with you. Married at seventeen,

widow at eighteen, husband snagged and leaking
on a barbed-wire fence in France. This half familiar
face, so innocent of what's to come, trials

and losses that sculpt the final visage, author
these hard-earned worry lines, eyes unaware
of all you've had to countenance. Who, indeed?

# Dale's Way

When not rowing his dinghy to the reef
to jig for cod or God, Dale holes up
in a cabin, working on his novel,
the one started in a Hell's Angels bar
in Saskatoon. Suspicious at first
of his pen and notepaper, the bikers

soon realize such tenacity requires
balls and declare him official writer
in residence. He's waiting for me now
in a wheelchair outside the hospice,
puffing a cigarette, unruly stories
stamping their feet, impatient to be

told. Before my ass grows numb
on the rough concrete garden slab
we roll into his palliative care room
with its chair, bed and well-worn copies
of the Bible and the *Dao De Jing.*
While Dale's solitary path resembled

the Way of Lao Tze, his inner strength
was of a different order. Threatened
to give up holiday time to support
striking fellow ferry workers or have
his nonconforming cabin reported
to authorities, Dale advised his boss

if he executed that unfair threat
to make damn sure he had plenty of fire
insurance. Son of a railway worker,
he grew up in a modest dwelling near
a market and library. He'd arrive
home with a dozen books in one hand;

in the other, a jar of crustaceans
in formaldehyde. Subaquatic
creatures and literary creation,
the two parallel tracks he followed,
kept to as staunchly as scriptures and
the enigmatic edicts of the *Dao*.

## For Ann

To say what I wanted
then, lilacs in bloom

along the avenues, you
laughing at my snail's

pace, striking up
conversations

with passing
or pissing

dogs. A day
without weather

or end. Gifts
of time and colour,

profligate
in their bestowal,

and needing no
further encouragement.

# By No Means Gone

*in memory of Eavan Boland*

Typing, infant on one knee, sights
trained on the canon and all that grates,
like the unintended irony in Yeats'
crass comment to the Scriblerus Club:

"Gentlemen, there are too many of us,"
not addressing the absence of women
but the surfeit of scribblers. An omen?
Yes, still no agency after fifty years

of suffrage. This is what you elected
to combat, to hold your ground,
to be taken seriously, to be found
without derision or surprise among

the gifted. You jockeyed between suburb
and city, between porridge and poem,
using the five-minute intervals. Home
meant more than nation. And your prime

movers? A rosy sleeper, a black lace fan,
small cries in the night. A dripping breast
was not a metaphor. You aced the test,
ran, meandered, walked but did not

waver. I think of the risks you took
to be participant rather than observer
in your poems, a welcome shit disturber
insisting that poets acknowledge their

ratio of power to powerlessness.
Dishes done, kids in bed, the rinse
cycle winding down, you refuse to mince
words with Smith Corona, tuck a shock

of unruly hair under your bandanna.
For you the major struggles lay inside
the family or body, in the wide
capacious classroom of the heart.

You urged a politics of equality
where the vulnerable went to the head
of the queue. The anorexic, you said,
hungers for recognition, but first

must vomit up nostalgia for the past.
More invested in a blackbird's broken
wing than in gunfire, shouts, or token
loyalties. For you the liberating

ordinariness of the object, or the act.
No ornament, no 'poetry,' thank you.
You oblige us all to weigh our words, chew
over our right to pen a piece like this.

# Goldstream

I stop to observe the salmon
spawn, thrusting urgent

egg-filled bodies against
the river's force, silver

scales discoloured, starving
to ensure the species'

future, flesh ragged around
the tail and lower body

from thrashing at gravel
to produce the hollowed

redd where egg
and sperm co-mingle,

a hedge to counter current
and predator — eagle, bear

or small fish darting underneath
to steal the roe. Fierce she is,

selective, urging on the chosen
male, that shadowing

shape, head and jaw deformed
but there to complete the job.

I turn back to the car. I, too,
have work to do, pressing

though not so seminal
or dramatic, my shrunken

face and slowing body
notwithstanding, these

tenuous texts shored up
against the wreckage.

# The Greenhouse Effect

*There's a certain liberation to be found
in bad taste. Art, like life, is a matter
of gifts, not refusals.*

— Patrick Grainville

## A Primer for Building

How thoroughly winter sun conducts
its rounds, inspecting timbered joints, locally
hewn cedar and balsam fir, recycled
windows and sliding-glass door that leave

behind a panorama of shifting reflections.
Notes, of course, are being taken: mistakes,
imperfections, light passing through cracks,
poor workmanship, elicit entrances

for bats and mice. Three rust resistant screws
have missed the mark entirely, their naked lengths
exiting the stud mid-way. As for drainage,
much could be said. And the largest window,

no joke, double-glazed but having lost
its seal, hasn't the foggiest notion how
to behave. Rounds over, will it survive?
Why not, it's warmer by degrees inside.

# Germination

Whose idea was this anyway? Who
planted the seed? Noah. Not the dude
with the ark; my stepson in Victoria
who has a snazzy wood and glass structure

in his backyard and an earlier slapdash
version on Galiano Island, both producing
like crazy. Whatever transpired, it must
be catching as a load of horse manure

has just arrived in my yard. I confess,
I never liked the story of the flood.
That boat could not have held matching
pairs of all the animals. An elephant

would have trashed the loading ramp
or put a foot through the deck. Giraffes?
Try navigating with two long necks
tangled in the sails and rigging. Start

with a seed the size of a needle's eye,
the kind no rich man can thread,
never mind pass through. This tiny
seed inspires more doubt than hope,

its journey begins in a plastic egg cup
in my south-facing bedroom window,
its dream of sweet red peppers
hanging like Christmas decorations.

Is it manufacturing oxygen yet?
What's worse, too little water or too
much? A plethora of parental concerns,
keeps me sleepless half the night. I wake

from visions of Jack and his beanstalk
and Voltaire's Pangloss who, facing chaos
and corruption, advised his few remaining
friends: *Il faut cultiver notre jardin.*

## Night Soil

I've watched the greenness vanish day
by day, so why not make a little home

for it to flourish in? My own small oxygen
factory, not much to set against the brutal

scale of clear-cut logging, here or in
the Amazon, but worth the gesture.

Meanwhile in my sun-rich bedroom,
I watch entranced as the first of those

improbable peppers thrusts its slim green
peeper from the soil like a periscope

and looks around, unimpressed by the pair
of dirty socks and Denver Hayes underwear

on the floor, a noisy alarm clock
and toilet smells drifting down the hall,

though I suspect some vestige of cellular
memory might have flashed the words

*night soil* in its slowly expanding brainpan.
I expect this bold explorer to do more

than vegetate and that its reconnaissance
take a literary turn, a touch of Dylan

Thomas and his green fuse revving for the race
ahead. If so, I'll offer thanks, sleep well.

## *Ay, there's the rub*

I, too, am tickled by tumultuous
rubs, the rough-hewn cedar boards
that form and frame this birthing
box and glass smoother than the flesh
of Jacob's cheek, the glissando slide
that conjoins notes sweet or discordant.

A tickling jest rubs me the wrong way
but only briefly. Holes in siding to be
quickly filled, boards not well aligned
to keep the nibblers out. I make exception
for the hummingbird, whose pointed
probing's needed and most welcome.

Green and golden I was until my mother
died. My fingers probed the fertile loam
that housed potato sprouts in matriarchal
soil. I did not find her there. Ripened
now and gone to seed, I sense her presence
in the work I do. Some call it husbandry.

# Hortus conclusus

Consider the greenhouse as anthology,
a gathering of possibilities, where
carrots, those control-freak sonneteers,

cohabit with free-verse peas that climb
the wall, or prosaic squash, those lovers
who spread out and colonize the bed.

The cast's inclusive, but structurally
challenged, which may explain the hammer
bludgeoning my green thumb blue.

My friend Bob, in China, tried to read
his *Seed Catalogue* to our bewildered
hosts, telling them how to grow a poet,

a prairie town or a first-class northern
bull-shitter. He was not big on symmetry,
controlled environments or cultural

revolutions, reminding us instead
of other options, like simple brome grass,
that 'Flourishes under absolute neglect.'

# The Rake's Progress

You think it's kid's stuff, mixing
seeds, words and rhymes in this
two-bit nursery, when a noun
like *fertilizer* can explode
in your face? Steer clear
of poet-gardeners, O.W. Toad
for starters, armed, arachnoid,
Mommy Long-legs, tending
her patch of carnivorous
plants, insane pioneers, toxic
geraniums. Keep a safe distance,
tend to your own plot.
Then there's foxy Levine
with his dark loam and raised bed
of missed opportunities,
non-compostable abstractions
like mercy, truth, a lost child
sucking his solitude because
that's all he has. This
is no Country Western, so
put your hoedown, avoid tools
of the trade, weed pullers,
trowels and claws that pursue
and sever living roots. Instruments
of torture, especially the rake,
which tries so hard and pointedly
to smooth things out, its row of metal
teeth enough to give a worm cardiac
arrest, or furrow a beetle's brow.

# Bare Bones

It's actually brown, not green, to match
the colours of the house, and erected
where the rotten deck once stood. I make

no claim to beauty or craftsmanship,
but think it adds a touch of clumsy grace
to an overlarge abode, a homely focus

like those old films that slowly morph
from wide pan to the solitary close-up
of a lighted window, where all that later

matters will take place. Self-exposure's
not the aim of art, or plants, but mutual
nourishment. Klein's fabled city is there

to recall, or imagine, opening our hearts
to the world once more, his green
inventory overlong in coming. I wake

with Roethke, taking it slow, knowing
other things that nature has in store.
The lovely bones are here to celebrate

if you ignore the distance between heron
and hawk and hold the summer in reserve,
mouthing platitudes of love and growth.

# By Any Other Name

All the big things happen in gardens
Pablo thinks, including that memorable
scene in Eden, after the naming of
species. He sits amidst his roses, feeling
horny as he ponders *Romeo and Juliet*.

What's in a name, Mistress Lovely muses
from her balcony. Romeo watches unseen
from bushes below, thinking Why not?
This gal's not just a beauty, she's bright;
I'll change my name, but what will it be?

This is a nominally defining moment
for Pablo too. He takes his new surname
from Czech poet Jan Neruda, wears it
like a beloved scarf, writes energy-infused
poems in green ink as a personal symbol

of hope, lavish lyrics ranging from love
to history and, of course, politics,
for which he is exiled, then exalted.
No green giants existed then, jolly
or otherwise, and no Green Party,

though the Irish honoured St Patrick
by painting faces and roads the colour
of clover. Pablo spends more of his time
admiring old socks than celebrating
nature. He is obsessed with antiques,

carvings, memorabilia of the sea,
the best a full-breasted damsel astride
an ornate bowsprit. Yes, ambassador
to India, then France, even winning
the coveted Nobel Prize for Literature,

inspiring music, films, a battalion
of imitators, all this taking place
while his old name Neftalí Ricardo
Reyes Basoalto grows pale and green
about the gills, then brown as winter grass.

# Bioaesthetics

A rose is a rose
as a stein is a stone

It emerges from seed
more or less on its own.

Yes, water assists
this solar translation

and Gertrude resists
abrupt immolation.

# The Beet Generation

the days of meat and potatoes
are coming to an end
howls of protest
                        notwithstanding

other forms of sustenance
emerge
                protean protein sources
bardic celebrations of hawthorn
berries for the heart
                        rosehip
tea for the stomach
with warnings to avoid
the small hairs that cause
an itchy anus

all this of interest to bearded
saints in the supermarkets
        of Frisco and Vancouver
                who bypass the central rows
        of canned and processed foods
hoping to avoid the cramp
of spirit
                prison of grammar,
regulations, laws, whatever
inhibits growth

and promotes the belated
merger of head and heart
                              that
corn-and-beans combo
that kept the Aztecs vital
and alive
                on the road or on
the warpath savouring
their naked
lunch

# Greenhouse Gases

When not constructing this cozy
cube I'm either walking with Ann
and my step-daughter Camas or talking
carbon dioxide, methane, nitrous oxide,

major heat-trapping gases that stabilize
the earth's temperature. Also joking about
my grade nine chemistry teacher
whose memory of elements was worse

than mine: You should know them by heart,
he insisted: neon, argon, krypton and
so on. Camas, an enthusiastic baker
who has just completed her master's

in Public History, is a professional
sceptic with a big heart. I thought, she says,
as we pass Glen's and Wendy's farm
on the narrow road to the steep north

of the island, that cows are the major
methane makers. Yes, I reply, nodding
to Basho, who is heading downhill
in baggy trousers and a conical straw hat.

Consumers of meat and the sourdough
bread you bake are significant contenders.
For proof, hang out in the greenhouse
in the first few hours after lunch.

# Going to Seed

Today Walcott is standing beside me
running his forefinger along the framed
edges of the triangular window
on the west side, smiling. Even alive,
he was not the talkative type, but he nods
his faint approval of the workmanship,
resisting the urge to be ironic. He knows
I've taken his measure, studied the poems,
essays, interviews. In "Early Pompeian,"
about the loss of a daughter, he wonders

why a seed would envy our desire
to "*flower, to suffer* and *to die.*" All this,
in an oeuvre replete with meditations
on change and loss, *hope of resurrection*
nil. And yet, he knows the heart *must
never harden.* Seeds, his own included,
have little to say about the path
ahead, the labours, the blights, the sharp
teeth and claws of nature and man, nothing
even the cutting-edge poem can protect

against, though words may be a soft
rain, a comforting warmth. My neighbour
Andy arrives with another pickup full
of oak leaves for mulching. I don't introduce
them, it would be too complicated. Good
work, says Homeric Derek, the *old brown man
in a moustache*, his quaint description of himself,
to me, a bearded white antiquity. Get on
with it, plant your perspicacious peppers
in a riot of nutrients. Good luck. And *Ciao*.

PS: I asked how a poem starts for him,
to which he replied: "It starts like everything
else that matters — people, chickens, plants
— there has to be an ovary action."

## Second Thoughts

It's not that I object to blight, which
has its own work to do, *capiche*? Oh ya,

fear of death persists, that silent driver
of decomposition, so I batten down hatches,
screen all callers, making my sterile

ward inviolable, immune. Even
bees and birds, those tireless little sex
workers, hired to pollinate and please, must
wear masks, carry passports, visitor's

visas, work permits, whatever flattens
fun and regiments the delirious dance,
desire's honeycomb. George P. Elliott's
kissing man is jailed at last, put out

of circulation, along with the grace
he administers. Should I trash this
anal fortress, this naysayer's last resort,

this edifice of denial and — hell! —
let the boisterous, pulsing
world invade?

# The Greenhouse Effect

I sit on the deck just outside a rectangular
cooling vent, battery-driven drill in hand,
taking stock. If the metal screen were
in place, this spot would resemble

a confessional. I have my list of sins
ready. But truth is, I'm more animist
than Catholic. So Mother Earth, here's
what's troubling me. I'm addicted to fossil

fuels, although I recently purchased solar
panels. At best I'm a slipshod, reluctant
recycler. Once I poured surplus paint
and chemicals into the earth, not thinking

of the water table. Is there hope for me?
What else? Well, sure, my human relations
record is not great, but I'd rather skip
the details. Three Heil Hitlers, you say?

Come on, I'm not that bad. A few lies,
contraband sex, a life or two interrupted
along the way. With this record, will any
self-respecting seed produce on my behalf?

Gary Geddes

I hadn't thought of that. I've been reading
about mycelium, the interconnectedness
of all things. I'm ready to reform, this
greenhouse my first big effort at contrition.

I cast my eye along the cedar siding,
the drill heavy, surprised this personal
garbage has emerged. That's when I see it,
halfway down the board: a screw loose.

# Codgertation

I linger in the empty space
to test its warmth, temperature
outside hovering around zero,

and take the measurements
for shelves, scent of cedar
still strong despite the stain

and condensation from the glass
roof. Will there be generating
particles from which things

grow here? *Ex nihilo fecit*, whisper
the boards, and I think at once
of the ubiquitous blank screen

or page. I need to understand
the poetics of this space, the lyric
line broken by desire, the heroic

coupling of emotion, idea, event,
the poem itself a small abode
of possibility, a semi-controlled

environment where surprise
is welcome, and where anything
can happen, including changes

in humidity, cross pollination,
judicial juxtapositions, exotic
etymologies, and playful shifts

of light that cultivate a certain
attitude or turn of phrase. A drop
of water settles on my baseball cap.

# Mourning Dove

A mourning dove alights on the glass
roof of the greenhouse. I'm inside
working on a small vent. I recognize
the long tail, buff colour, black smudges
on white-tipped wings. Hi Rita, I say,
I wasn't expecting you, but welcome
just the same. To what do I owe my good
fortune? As you're not the visitation
of a deceased relative, you must be
a visiting angel, a harbinger of good
news. Unlike your secret garden, mine's
an open book, nothing to hide but shoddy
workmanship. The cucumbers and kale
are glad you're here to ride herd, make sure
things go according to Hoyle. Rita knows
this is hype, or bullshit, that nothing
I do is by the book. She lifts her elegant
tail and drops a compliment atop the glass.

# Garden Varieties

One species just not welcome
here is Lilburn's preposterous
pumpkin, with its boisterous
belly laugh and Texas appetite.

We'll teach it not to be here,
but elsewhere, the community
garden perhaps, where excess
spreads at leisure like a virus.

To start, we'll privilege the lyric
voice, celebrate the power
of metaphor and music. A bit
tight-assed, I admit. Okay, I'll

make room for story too, accept
good advice from the ancient
Buddhist scribe who advised,
in a manuscript long hidden

in the secret Library Cave
in Dunhuang, an oasis town
near Singing Sand Mountain,
where routes of the Silk Road

merge at the easternmost edge
of the Taklamakan Desert.
*Sing as if narrating*, he advised,
and *narrate as if singing.*

Paul Robeson tomatoes will
be given priority, of course,
his golden voice enough
to make veggies rise up

determined to strut their
stuff. His anti-racist and anti-
capitalist narrative leaves
no room for the co-called

Moneymaker tomato, just
as it requires altered lyrics
for the Showboat musical's
hit song, Old Man River.

I know you're thinking: what
happened to standards in this
unrhymed extravaganza? Do I
contradict myself? Very well then ...

# *Veggierotics*

This will be my garden of earthy
delights, modest, given more
to culinary than erotic excess:
basil, mint, varieties of broccoli,

cilantro, kale for my drop-dead
pesto. My project, frugal
in scale, will hardly interest
Mr. Bosch with his hellish

triptych on the loss of innocence.
No hijinks here or group sex,
only the fitful fumbling of tiny
feelers in pollen, pistil and stamen.

I'd like to ask Hieronymus
about the large spiked blue
ball in the central panel that
resembles a World War II

naval mine, as I hope to specialize
in explosive tastes, the kind
that make your mouth water, your
heartbeat quicken. Before passing

judgement, drop in to catch a whiff
of fragrances emitted by heady
herbs and citrusy oils, stored in
the hairy trichomes of tomato plants.

## Ode for Services

Always the desire to write something
light but lyrical, the kind of dance
that makes us all want to stand up
loose-limbed and boogie, or drift
like tumbleweed across the living-room

floor to soft music, lush memories
spreading over membranes smooth
as fresh cream. Or just enjoy the silken
folds of silence. It's not too much to ask.
You know that, sitting at your makeshift

desk in the back bedroom, tea cooling
in your favourite cup, the bulging blue
mug that holds the most, a roster of wrens
busy at the feeder. But your head
is full of the morning news, politics

below the 49th parallel, bellies
bloated from hunger in Yemen, pipelines
disgorging gunk in rivers and lakes,
boiled water advisories. You try
to blot it out, thumbing your favourite

texts, hoping a word or phrase will
attach itself like a burr, blot out
all the dreck. That's when you notice
the chestnut-backed chickadee alight
on a branch the shape of a pachyderm's

trunk. It preens a moment, brown waistcoat,
grey trim of wings, black and white markings
there and on the head, delicate triangle
of beak. The perfect English gentleman,
a winged version of Little Lord Fauntleroy

without the decadence and self-importance.
It deposits a roasted sunflower seed on the bark,
working it into bite-sized pieces, the song
its onomatopoeic name, enough
to inspire this manic-depressive ode.

## *Joinery*

Father, I've kept a place for you among
the poets. You had an affinity for wood,
whether cutting poplars to provide winter
fuel or shaping barns and boats. Though
you never wrote or recited a line of verse,
you understood the tortured syntax
of arbutus, the subtle sibilance of cedar.
You never used a scriber or a square
to cut a straight line, pungent sawdust
rising from the board. I held your hand
and sang while you were dying. I make
this modest tribute to your craftsmanship,
a joiner of words to a joiner of wood.
This tiny shed's a shelter for you now.

# Family Matters

*They fuck you up, your mum and dad.*
*They may not mean to, but they do.*

— PHILIP LARKIN

# *Peleus*

I never loved Astydameia, could tolerate her
only in bits and pieces. So when the lie she told
caused Antigone to hang herself, I dispatched
the bitch and drove my horses and chariot
over her prostrate body. Not a proud moment

for a would-be hero, an Argonaut sent in pursuit
of the golden fleece. I was also a member
of the hunt for the Calydonian Boar, a beast
of mythic proportions whose ravages
laid waste the harvest and its crew of threshers

and dogs. Two surprises during that hunt:
spearing my stepfather Eurytion by accident,
impetuous behaviour that prompted my flight
from Phthia; and, second, would-be champions
bested in the hunt by the woman Atalanta,

who drew first blood. The ensuing free-for-all
took countless lives, including Meleagros,
the king's son. My wife dead, costly theatrics
taking their toll, a career change was what
I needed most. Zeus, mischief-maker and

destiny-weaver, had plans for this newly
unemployed mortal involving a mate
for Thetis—she whom no god would marry
because of succession prophecy: a son
who would outshine his father. He made

me an offer I could not refuse. Poseidon,
his water-logged brother, assigned the sea-god
Proteus to advise me in the ways and
wiles of Thetis, who rejected my offer
as beneath her rank. A forced union

not to my liking, but I took his advice,
binding the lovely shape-shifter in her sleep.
Angry but subdued, she consented. After
feasting, gifts of two immortal horses
and an ashen spear forged by Hephaestus,

I was almost too potted to perform,
but the deed was done, Achilles' seed planted,
a boy half-god half-man. What followed
was not a time to rejoice and celebrate.
Thetis harnessed the elements to purge

our child of mortal flesh. To protect him
from his own mother, I placed the boy
in the caring hands of Chiron, who trained
him in the arts of medicine and war, myself
in the management of grief and shame.

# A Bad Rap for Thetis

What can I say that you don't already
know? My marriage to mortal Peleus
was not forced, neither was it an act

of passion. Something in the bones
confirmed it important, foreordained.
I knew bugger-all about genetics,

that the half-mortal issue of my loins
would leave an open wound, render me
vulnerable. Some argue I helped

release Prometheus from his chains, took
pleasure with Diomedes in a bed of seaweed,
refused to save a boy from drowning

in a shipwreck. These are mostly lies.
I admit a modicum of shape-shifting
to avoid capture, goddess of water

employing the other elements, winging
it, assuming fiery shapes and ground-breaking
disguises to achieve my ends. Immortal

perks I wanted for my son Achilles
when I dunked him headfirst in the toxic
waters of the Styx. Who'd have guessed

forefinger and thumb that kept him
submerged would guarantee the weakness
leading to his death, my loss, and change

the crazy, cockeyed course of history?
Divine intervention's no mere literary
device. It's true I like to hang out with

live-aboards and lowlifes at marinas,
sharing their love of all that floats or swims,
as well as strong libations. If you should

see me depicted riding the sea nymph
Hippokampos, Achilles' shield on my right
arm, or choose to believe the lament

of kingfisher that I cut off cod stocks,
don't be too judgemental. Remember:
mothers are bound to mourn, the oysters

I bring to banquets are tastier than
truffles, and Apollo sang at my wedding,
his honeyed lyrics blessing all creation.

# *Achilles*

What future's to be found in valiant
deeds if the hero's name conjures
weakness, tendons the target of crude
laughter? While etymologists dither

over the meaning and origin of words,
whether they signify glory or guilt,
let me assure you nature and nurture
are both culprits here. The simple truth:

family matters. My father Peleus,
King of Myrmidons, is a rough diamond
who took no prisoners, so I come by the phrase
'wrath of Achilles' quite naturally. Mother,

a goddess who married beneath her rank,
was not inclined to tolerate human
foibles, though they mirror divine chaos.
She kept me occupied with music lessons

taught by a centaur of good heart, bad
breath. It's said she tried to burn away
my mortal flesh as an infant, holding me
over flames. Of that I have no memory

or scars, though it may explain my hot
temper. You might expect a sea nymph's son
to have, like Ulysses, a penchant for sailing,
but fifty ships later and I still quake

at large bodies of water. Proof she almost
drowned me in the river Styx? Easily
distracted she was. Consider my parents
whacko, but keep in mind my extended

family, the gods. When Agamemnon
refused to give up Chryseis as his concubine,
short-fused Apollo responded with a plague, a deal
that cost me lovely the Briseis. Enraged,

I went on strike, holed up in my tent,
Patroclus pleading as fortunes of war
shifted in the Trojan's favour. I loaned him
my shield and armour as a ruse, but Hector

slew him, aided by that horny pack
of egotists with celestial real estate.
Don't get me started on bloodlines
lest poison pens inscribe. I'm out of here.

## Patroclus

I've been called the lover of Achilles,
comforter of doleful Briseis,
and a man unfit to wear the hero's
armour. Regarding the first accusation,
I'd gladly have given my friend

anything he desired, but we remained
comrades-in-arms, not intimates.
His father Peleus raised me, hot-headed
as I was. Gentle Chiron tutored me,
made me a fit companion. I don't mind

admitting battlefields ran with the blood
of Trojans and their allies, including
noble Sarpedon, the favourite son
of Zeus. Persuaded not to favour progeny,
Zeus sent rain instead of lightning

on the Trojan heads. But when my spear
released Sarpedon's spirit, Apollo,
incensed, addled my brain, making me
easy work for Hector's fatal thrust.
Argue I was Achilles' alter ego

if you must, providing the tenderness
he lacked, whatever theory satisfies
your ache for order. My solace lies
in knowing those who truly cared for me
shed hair and let my ashes burn their hands.

# Hector

I preferred playing with my son
Astyanax to dispatching

Greeks. The little moppet with
his delicate fingers, soft

heart, who wept to see a bird
taken, a stray dog crushed

beneath chariot wheels. We chucked
pebbles in the river Scamander,

whose name he bears and whose
blood ran just as pure. I recall

his fright at my helmet's
reflected glow — did he see

the future imaged there?
Too soon discovered hiding

in his father's tomb, fair game
for Neoptolomus, his bloody maw.

Revenge is undignified,
unholy. And Andromache,

who fought to save our son,
was forced to be his killer's

concubine, Priam begging
for my body or its parts. Paris

grooming himself for action,
agent of gods whose sport

this is. It spreads, diplomacy
a dying art, decency close behind.

# Zeus Agonistes

Mixed signals here. Achilles asked
his mother Thetis to implore me
on behalf of enemies. She, for whom

I lusted, was difficult to refuse,
so I let Trojans drive the superior Greeks
back to their ships, just far enough

to arouse Achilles' anger, and get him
out of bed. I do tire of all these pleas
and petitions, mortals and gods

begging me to intervene. All this over
sexy Helen whose beauty will be said
to launch a thousand hips. Ha, ha.

The carnage mounts. At least it's honest
face-to-face ferocity, the clean thrust
that separates head and torso, a little

dirty-work thrown in by me in my role
as *deus ex machine.* At times I wonder
about fate. Do gods have agency?

Are we too slaves of destiny? Oracles
know more than I do, even with my nest
of spies, under-the-counter intelligence.

Am I foreordained to interfere
in mortal affairs? Should I consult a shrink?
Too many questions, but one thing's

certain: there's a crucial difference
between omniscience and omnipotence.
Get my drift? Let that, at least, be known.

# Chiron

My father Kronos, another shape-shifter,
took to horsing around with the sea nymph
Philyra. So why aren't you half fish,
friends ask, instead of this human body
with equine legs and posterior?

Search me. The Old Man is said to have
castrated his father and devoured his own
offspring lest they do the same. I'm proof
those stories are not factual. Dimwitted
literalists always screw things up;

Kronos's scythe symbolizes harvest,
a simple instrument for releasing seed.
Unlike other centaurs, heads in the temple,
asses in the gutter, I had the luxury
of dabbling in music, agriculture,

medicine and the martial arts. I taught
archery and specialized in healing
herbs. My role as Achilles' tutor had
its challenges, namely opposing views
of education. Pugnacious but well

intentioned, Peleus favoured a more
liberal approach, while Thetis, out of fear,
chose to protect her son, keep him under
wraps, more conservative by a mile.
Say you got it from the horse's mouth,

not his other orifice. As one who cherishes
his feminine side, I taught Achilles
and Patroclus to be sensitive, athletic,
strong. I took pride in my modest success,
not that it made much difference in the end.

# Briseis

It's fair to say I had a literary bent,
tossed off poems and plays to be dismissed
by critics. Aeschylus tried to explain

that conversation is not quite the stuff
of drama; only dialogue has roots deep
in character and conflict. Piffle. I had

to laugh, this from the grand master
of the monologue, speeches long enough
to make cows weep. Human psychology

was my ticket. I was a bit player
in the Homeric legend, my sky-blue eyes
and unruly hair currency enough

to attract Achilles. After he'd killed
my entire family, including Mynes,
a husband more moth than butterfly,

Achilles took me as his prize. How to
endure the touch of a murderer, even
a handsome one? Women learn to adapt

quickly, as whores to unloved husbands.
The sex was good, a man trained to use
his tongue more than his tool is hard

to find. From his sad, shy expression
as he watched me disrobe in the half
light, I augured he'd come to love me

enough to weep with rage when I was
reassigned to aged Agamemnon, inept
in all but war. Without Achilles,

the battle would be lost. Negotiations
ensued. Aggie's gifts refused, our hero
spurred to action only by the death

of Patroclus. In victory he was mine,
however brief those fugitive hours.
I prepared, in grief, his perfect body

for the afterlife, my tears comingled
with his blood. Poised to be consigned
again: rejected manuscript, dented shield.

# Chorus Line

Of love we sing, its rich
dubiety. Relationships,

those floundering vessels,
how they list to port.

Of love we warble, its
multiple shades.

Patroclus, Achilles, devoted
they were, and tender.

We have a word for this:
*hetairos*, the love of comrades

who sleep with women
but prefer each other's

company. Patroclus, older,
gave himself less

to moods or whims, and left
theatrics to his fated

friend. So what's the latest
scoop? Of love we

croon, its shades divinely
criminal.

Our hero, spoiled, used
to being served,

was neither vassal nor vizier
to the flowery combat

of sex. Yet he acknowledged
the ache of immortals

to know the pangs of passion,
the sting of loss.

# Kingfisher's Lament

You'll not catch me napping on a stump
or piece of driftwood, white throat bared
to the knife or rake of an eagle's talons.
More cautious, I slip out of sight
in the dappled light of the rain forest,
my streamlined body tucked between
overlapping boughs of cedar. You imagine
it's sleep I enact in the stillness of the trees,
or a ritual of submission and respect
for the upright giants. No, it's to distract

predators from my burrow amongst the reeds
and sandy banks. You hear my rattle to your left
before the flash of turquoise wings is seen,
wonder if there's truth in rumours that I nest
at sea and Thetis pacifies winter storms
at incubation time. The Greeks thought so,
giving my name to the halcyon peace and calm
associated with childhood. Aeolus, my father,
deserves the credit for placid waters. Silver-
footed Thetis, she of the lovely hair,

I blame for scattering my darlings, shivering
in their nests. Others accuse her falsely
for the disappearance of herring. She saved
and nurtured Hephaistos, cast out by his own
mother for being lame, offered him refuge,
rejoiced at his gifts as a smith, forge and tongs
effecting a craftsman's alchemy. By all accounts,
examples of her care and good advice are legion.
Fierce she was to save Achilles' life, trained him
in womanly garb and wiles to dwell among

the maidens. But enough of that, this is *my* story,
I Alcyone, who found my husband drowned
and cast my body in the sea to share
his fate. The gods rewarded my devotion,
turned me into a kingfisher, one who forever
plunges in search of the beloved. I'm purported
to be a good omen, protector of mountains
and springs, a minor deity. Rubbish, just poets
taking liberties. I'm stockier now, white scarf,
slate-blue wings, rufous band around my belly.

# Peripatetic

*The world is a book, and those who do not travel read only one page.*

— Saint Augustine

# Northwest Passage

As the raft moves downriver, inflatable
but not, alas, indestructible, we adjust
our bodies, feet thrust under the luggage
rack for stability, paddles at the ready, rain

looking for cracks in all-weather gear,
determined to dampen clothes or spirits
on this journey from the Firth headwaters
to the Beaufort Sea. Merv's in the stern,

not thinking of tent circles or carbon-dated
artefacts that go back 10,000 years. Instead,
he's concerned with water samples that might
indicate the presence of toxins, mercury

from the melting permafrost. His Parks
Canada jacket has a broken zipper.
Merv shrugs. He's done this trip fifty times,
accompanied or alone, and prefers winter

when the snowmobile moves with ease
over river ice and drifting snow and
a broken zipper means death. Months
of midnight sun don't faze Merv. He jokes

of how his wife, before sending him off,
always says, make sure you're home before dark.
Tonight in the Marmot, our communal tent,
he recalls his ancestors, moving back

and forth along the Alaska/Yukon coast,
following game, epic undertakings
he considers old-hat. We're on alert
for wildlife, moose, caribou, muskox,

the elusive wolverine. All we've managed
so far are Dall sheep and the ubiquitous
sic-sics, arctic gophers with a penchant
for dry suits, rubber boots, unofficial

agents of the duct-tape industry. No
grizzlies spotted yet but fresh scat and tracks
evident, so they know our whereabouts,
those lengthy claws for digging roots.

We sing *Day-o, / Say day-ay-ay-o*
as we bushwhack to avoid surprising
mother and cubs. No Belafontes
in the group, more fear than frivolity

in our chorus. Stan Rogers is with us
too, in haunting lyrics about the doomed
and hapless Franklin, trying to surpass
his knighthood and cruel governorship

in Tasmania with a coup in Canada's
north, in command of *Erebus*, a ship
whose name conjures it all: a mythical
being, born of chaos. The wreck found

a hundred and sixty-nine years later
with Inuit help in the depths of Queen Maud
Sound. Malnutrition, lead poisoning, plus
evidence of cut marks on human bones.

## David's Poem

David's mother kneels
beside the seal hole,
no existential angst
gnawing at her solar

plexus, just the comforting
drumbeat of her heart.
Food for the months
ahead, necessity bred

in the bone. Spear
in one hand, baited line
in the other, she crouches
motionless, alert to the

slightest movement
in the water below. Wind
has picked up, the brief
gift of daylight almost

spent. Alone on the ice.
Blowing snow slants across
her vision, whittles the drifts,
its song plaintive, gossamer

thin. A rank whiff, just enough,
reaches her first. Without
hesitating, she whirls about
and drives a mitted fist

into the open mouth
of the surprised bear.
The creature, a white
storm rising to its full

nine feet of intensity,
staggers back, emits
a choked guttural
growl, collapses on ice.

No seal, she reports
back home, only a dead
*nanuq*, fish-skin mitten
stuck in its throat.

## Sheep Slot Rapids

Olivia inches along the rocky outcrop,
camera in hand, bent on recording
the transit of inflated rafts through Sheep
Slot Rapids, the narrows boiling ashen
white, an eight-foot drop enough to swallow

kayak or canoe. Neil, head guide,
commands the raft's long oars
as it jockeys the swift glacial flow.
Rich and Jeff in stern, paddles ready
to resist the deadly tug of rock or snag.

While we portage the craggy bluff,
Olivia stations herself on the nearest
ledge to record each deft manoeuvre,
lead raft laden with half a ton of gear,
a thick carpet draped like armour over

the bow. Prostrate on a horizontal
slab, she frames the scene, zooms in to film
the muscles in each face, contorted
and intense as they assess the torrent's
grip, both paddles driven down

in frantic snatches to prevent the stern
from taking the lead in this mad birthing
moment, when the slightest lapse might
spell disaster. Camera steadied on granite
she struggles to dismiss distracting thoughts:

an ageing mother's frailty in the face
of rushing time, her own husband swept
away untimely by disease. Starboard oar
nudges a protruding tusk of rock and lifts
Neil off his seat, threatening to breech

the narrows, but the two paddlers thrash
and tear at froth, bring the stern into line
and the raft pops like a cork through the gap,
umbilical stern rope trailing behind, our
wild applause overwhelmed by turbulence.

# Quintet in Sea Minor

## 1.

Neither the thin blue stripe
of his overalls, dark shadows
under his chin, nor the game

light plays with surfaces
holds my attention. Not even
the drum with its heavy

strands of net, and ellipsis
of white cork floats. But
something in the eyes

of this man on the afterdeck
of an Alaskan seiner hints
at more that must be said:

the ubiquitous failure of words.
But what has this to do with me?
I didn't take the photograph

or give it to the archive. A spouse,
perhaps, or lover, wondering how
long this time, supplies lowered

on pallets from the pier. I should
stick to music, blues reflective
of my present frame of mind.

2.

*Camera in hand, she observes its cautious*
*descent. Plump belly, long thin tapered tail*
*hugging the creosoted piling. Pause,*
*head turns, whiskers and grey nose twitch, reach*
*out to gather in the fugitive aromas*
*of food, the latent danger. They'll share*
*this trip, she realizes, rough seas,*
*perilous conditions, delicate feet*
*inching along planks and ribs for scraps*
*until the sack of rice is located. Then*
*it's just the business of avoiding*
*traps, slicing the thick cotton weave to carry*
*off and stash away the rich brown grains.*
*Shipmates, sharing food, accommodation,*
*DNA, mutual distrust, hostages*
*to weather, chance and, yet, in the end, as*
*interdependent as lovers. Lucky rat.*

3.

*Back at the flat, she extracts the cartridge*
*of film, sets it on the windowsill behind*
*the kitchen sink. A grim light clings to the*
*brick walk-up next door, renders the wilting*
*spider plant more pathetic, its faded*
*chlorophyll pigments scarcely deserving*
*the descriptor green. Neither she nor the plant*
*will absorb much energy from the sun*
*in the weeks ahead. 'Green around the gills,'*
*that quirky phrase flits across her brainpan,*

*elicits a sad smile, huge sigh and impulse*
*to kick his wayward slipper so it arcs*
*over rumpled bedclothes to alight*
*on a pile of unwashed laundry. So what's*
*the fuss, he's not gone off to war*
*or shacked up with someone else. He'll*
*return fatigued, smelling of diesel, fish.*

4.

*She switches on the darkroom's red light,*
*the developing paper less sensitive*
*to longer wavelengths. Burning is required*
*for contrast, to accentuate the face, and*
*dodging to soften details of cabin*
*and deck clutter, her magician's fingers*
*enhancing or inhibiting exposure. Better*
*to marry than burn, words from the past,*
*pulpit words, verbal associations*
*still present. Even with separations*
*like this, the burn continues. Work, yes,*
*keep yourself busy, dodging temptation.*
*Or not. Like Jack Dawkins in Dickens'*
*book <u>Oliver Twist</u>, the Artful Dodger.*

5.

That photo in the archives
made me weep. A minor
chord, as if foreknowledge

were involved, a face I'd never
seen before but somehow
knew. I don't believe in past

lives, though cellular memory
makes a kind of sense,
trauma-inscribed cells, now

called epigenetic inheritance.
Hands so expressive, yet thrust
deep in his pockets lest they

reveal too much. Disarmed?
Shorthanded? Forgive the puns.
I'm talking marks or tags

that don't alter genetic
sequencing, but change the way
they play out, as female

rodents forget to reduce
stress by licking
their young.

# The Lord's Work in Uganda

## Case One

Rebels caught us in the garden between rows
of cabbage and sorghum. The men, my husband
included, were grabbed and beaten, the rest of us
forced to climb a rocky incline until our knees

were shredded to the bone. On pain of death,
I killed my husband while the children watched.
Aid workers fled the village. A second group
of rebels killed my mom and elder brother.

Swelling was painless at first, then the leg
grew large and hurt like hell. My son dropped out
of Senior One and now burns charcoal. I got
another man and two more kids, but then he left.

## Case Two

Mostly, I'm silent now. Rituals of cleansing
did not work. Mine was a leper's welcome.
My husband can't stop thinking of the older
men I was given to, Kony's people. Abducted

three times, age seven to fourteen. Kill or be killed,
the rebels said. Mother, father, forgive me.
The village was on a small river by the border.
A rebel appeared in the doorway. He'd used

a rope to pull himself across during the flood.
I carried his looted property, then his child.
Nothing's smooth; it's jagged, like this bottle cap
I shift from hand to hand. Of course, I'm bitter.


*Case Three*
We mutilate but spare the pregnant ones,
the rebels explained. The others must be
killed. I never understood the logic.
When they cut off my ears, nose and lips,

my gutless husband couldn't bear
to look at me. A government soldier
posted elsewhere, he has another wife
now. Anger? I had to let that go; it

would have finished me. And justice,
what's that? Abducted boys in posh
jail cells in The Hague, clutching a
remote control instead of an AK-47?

## All About Love

Some kinds of travel
require so little exertion,
lips silently shaping

and reshaping thought, eyes
closed, seeing more
clearly that way, auditory

antennae on reduced
alert in their chambers
of cartilage and bone,

all this time the tongue
having the good taste
and sense not to wag,

skin taking it all in,
and all in good form.
Travelling light

it's called, mental
baggage stowed away
in a distant locker,

key out of reach,
not even the smell
of burning forests

or flesh can disturb
or distract you now, nasal
passages desensitized

by tobacco or cocaine. Tune it
out, the guru whispers
in a voice almost

hypnotic, one hand
on your crotch, the other
on your wallet, while

someone in a nearby room
draws the delicate hairs
of a bow over catgut

and drowns out a child's
cry, traffic's hum, planet's
final gasp and wheeze.

# Le jardin du Vaucluse

## 1. Bookworm

*Mais oui,* the Sorgue borders Petrarch's garden,
fed by springs that wind for miles beneath
the limestone hills, then surface in Vaucluse.
Like poetry or love you can't tell where

it originates or when it might burst
forth, gushing one day, dormant the next.
Intermittent, *le mot juste* for the Laura
syndrome. Rise and fall of her bosom

barely perceptible across the aisle,
two pews back. The sermon in Latin, bone-
dry, addresses the flesh and its desires.
As she senses his gaze — this stranger who

it's said buries his nose in manuscripts —
Petrarch ponders her discomfort, her blush.

## 2. Honey

She feels the slow worm stir between her thighs,
registering heat, pulse, blood-pool haywire.
If now the priest should call on her to stand
she would cry out as if the Holy Ghost

or some other had entered her body.
Grace? Possession? At best ambivalence.
Sly, dervish, a mistral boogies the Sorgue,
distorting twelve reflected shapes, boxes

you'd not suspect of being industries:
bee-hives, clean, compact as city-states, each
equipped with drones, queen. Previously warned,
Petrarch's family fled the plague. Dante

too, though he did not escape reprisals.
A bee hovers, precious cargo intact.


*3. Mother's Milk*

What thoughts occupy this pair as worm turns,
as bee poises aloft? Adjust bonnet,
feign concern for the sleeping child. Resist,
lest you give away too much, this stranger's

gaze. To employ the old vernacular,
as the poet insists, she *needs must know*
if all's imagined, if the ravages
of birthing have opened her to wayward

thoughts, fleshly ambitions. The infant's
forehead grazes her nipple; he has nodded
off with half the congregation. The poet
also bows, prayer the last thing on his mind.

He scribbles a few notes in the small book
kept in the pocket of his tunic, smiles.

## 4. *Fleas*

If he'd held my gaze, it would have been
different, she thinks. Adultery, flight,
the hiring of nannies. Nothing so fine
as unrequited lust, he jots down. Church

deprives a man of mountains, a picnic
with friends beside the river. But politics
behooves attendance, sì? A modest price
for appearances, privilege, travel.

Should Rome beckon, he'll exchange Laura
for laurels. Had she suspected, body
in revolt from convention, soul risking
perdition, might she have cursed poetry,

Petrarch, God and, hastening her demise,
called down plague on all their houses?

## 5. *Slight List to Port*

He dreams of galleys driven by desire,
storms of passion, treacherous shoals, rope enough
to keelhaul himself. The vessel of love
wallows in self-pity. Alternatives

occur: commerce, other women. Of course
he knows a good thing when he sees it.
More mileage in Laura than in a legion
of pale abstractions. He sniffs the makings

of a great poem, steady employment
with all the benefits, few of the costs,
tears enough to blind a crocodile.
Poor Laura, what's required of you? To be

out of reach, to burn for this cunt-teaser,
this famous poet with a pen for prick.

# The Shaving-Brush Tree
## a.k.a. pseudobombax ellipticum

With track-lights overhead, this Latin
porn star seems
too shy
to strut its stuff.
Not a leaf in sight,
it trembles as café
customers, bent
over salsa and tacos,
grumble and fart
in the warm night
air. No gallows
tree or crucifix,
nothing
false, pretentious
or bombastic
about this naked
loner, this ad for
privacy, doing
its thing with
no music,
no fanfare, not even
a Canada Council
grant.
But look, the show
has just begun.
Delicate foreskins
peel back, sprays
of white hair
glisten in

reflected light,
slender pink
pistils thrust their
glans or stigmas
into the receptive
night air. Police
sirens resound in
the distance,
grow louder.
Close
shave? Patrons
oblivious, lost
in small
talk, don't
notice the erotic
display, this
trotting
out of wares, or
unawares, if not
its whens and
whys. Nightly,
Gabriel and
other
angels, shake
themselves
awake,
douse armpits
with deodorant
and drag
their unsexed bodies
down from
heaven for the
show

# Royal Flush

Up here the air grows thin, breathing
laboured, steps plodding Too little
oxygen reaches the brain and other
organs. At sea-level, as the doctor

tried to explain, permeable cells
draw in weighty molecules on behalf
of the vascular system. Now they're
under strain, disabled at this altitude.

I doubted a guide necessary,
except to employ locals, but the slow
pace established makes sense,
stopping to discuss Oyama firs

with the 'Christian' cross at branch
tips. Like butterflies, the trees prefer
the cool sustaining mists up here.
As we slowly climb the sanctuary trail

nothing prepares us for the deluge
of colour that sweeps over us, bright
orange wing-tips outlined in black,
a constellation of tiny stained-glass

windows. Hundreds of multi-hued
creatures make temporary landings
on my clothes and arms, transform
my straw hat into a crown or exotic

head-dress so I resemble jester,
king or 12-star general, be-medalled
and bedazzled. Other mariposas
pause on the path just long enough

to drink or copulate, lift off again
with probable smiles on implausible
lips. The fourth generation lives
longest: egg, caterpillar, chrysalis,

adult butterfly, not seven ages
but multiple stages of silken
metamorphosis. While scientists
debate its dependence on weather

or smell, this inveterate voyageur,
threatened by development, pesticides
and illegal logging in the sanctuary,
navigates without GPS or flight

simulator thousands of kilometres.
I think of my friend Homero, poet,
former Mexican ambassador and
founding member of Grupo Cien,

dedicated to protecting endangered
species and their habitats, forced
to hire armed bodyguards. I'll plant
a field of milkweed just for him.

# The Right Words

*for Billy Collins*

So keen to visit Istanbul he can't refuse
        the offer of a few extra days.
                He wants to see where Trotsky stayed

in Prinkipo after his exile from Russia
        and the school his friend Gök attended
                as a young Turk, a walled compound

from 1481 opening onto Istlikal Street.
        He stands in awe of its marble pillars,
                green iron gates with gold-tipped

torches, arrows, trumpets and crossed swords.
        Images of that trip cling to his brain
                like barnacle encrustations, but nothing

so much as the ancient baths that scrubbed
        clean the sweat and dead skin of sultans, his
                too. So when he finds the famous poet's

piece on Istanbul, and its rich tribute
        to those who care for the feet and wellbeing
                of strangers, he is so taken with the words

he summons the courage to interrupt
        his wife's dinner preparations, a ritual
                not to be taken lightly. He starts to share

that poem but can't finish for weeping
        at the beauty of its final lines, which
                takes him back six decades

to the moment his Milton professor broke
        down reading *Paradise Regained* aloud
                and had to leave the classroom to regain

his composure. Right words in the right
        order. Better, the poet said, to be face down
                in warm soap suds than *facedown in a warm*

*pool of blood,* a sentiment even Trotsky
        would have endorsed, before the infamous
                ice-axe etched its sorry syntax into history.

# Afterword

~

Yes, this is a mixed bag, a modest offering of what was allowed by a hard-headed muse, ticked off with me for a ten-year dalliance with prose non-fiction. She made me sit up and beg or fight for every phrase and line, which may explain the shifts in mood, quality and content. I don't apologize for diversity, as books of 'occasional verse' used to be the norm; although, having written so many book-length poetic narratives and thematically uniform poem-sequences, even I am surprised by the variety here. I hope you'll find enough well made pieces to justify the gift of your attention. What follows are a few afterthoughts on the manuscript.

I saw my first termite mound in Somaliland, in an arid landscape dotted with abandoned tanks, ordnance and the occasional stray camel. It resembled, in the distance, a ghostly human form, but was actually a hive of living activity. I wondered what these voracious creatures ate other than wood. Is that why there wasn't a single house or dwelling to be seen? During the decade that followed, there were many losses in my life, relatives, close friends, some of my literary heroes. And, of course, the innocent victims of violence, greed and neglect. More than once I thought of those termites, and the gnawing effects of time itself, and recalled that compelling line in Beckett's *Waiting for Godot*: "We give birth astride of a grave." So short this life, which Nadine Gordimer likens to a flash of fireflies, a brevity to which only poems and short stories seem capable of doing justice. I've tried to celebrate those lost lives here in some small way, while taking refuge in the awe and wonder of a natural world under great duress.

"The Greenhouse Effect" is a term normally applied to the network of gases affecting and regulating the earth's atmosphere. However, in this case, it refers to the impact on me of spending three months trying to build a tiny greenhouse attached to south-facing back porch of my house. It was a challenge, alternately exciting and frustrating. I spent more time scratching my head pondering the mistakes I'd just made and wondering what to do next than actually building, all the while cursing myself for not paying more attention to my father, who had all the necessary skills. As the greenhouse emerged, more or less as planned, I found my head abuzz with images, anecdotes and metaphors about seeds, planting and growth, the small reward (or punishment) for a job only reasonably well done. Then various literary and artistic figures began to show up to inspect my labours or interrupt my thoughts and put in their two-cents' worth on gardening, flowers and life: Theodore Roethke, A.M. Klein reciting excerpts from his famous "Portrait of the Poet As Landscape," Dylan Thomas, Pangloss from Voltaire's *Candide*, Ginsberg, Kerouac and the howling Beats, Philip Levine, Margaret Atwood, Gaston Bachelard, Rita Dove, Robert Kroetsch,

Gertrude Stein, the two painters William Hogarth and Hieronymus Bosch, Pablo Neruda, Derek Walcott, Tim Lilburn, Walt Whitman and, to add a second prosaic intruder, the novelist George P. Elliott, whose novel *The Kissing Man* has a central character whose name, strangely, is Geddes. With that plethora of scribblers crowding out my small greenhouse, and even smaller brain, you might justifiably wonder — if it's not too contrary — how does your garden possibly grow?

"Family Matters" began as a meditation after I moved to one of the smaller Gulf Islands called Thetis. The island is not named after the Greek marine goddess and mother of Achilles, but after the British warship that terrorized coastal Indigenous communities during the early colonial period. Years before moving to Thetis Island, I had participated in a poetry and history conference at Sterling University in Scotland and spent half the night dancing to wild and wonderful music at a ceilidh, and imbibing too much single malt scotch. I awoke the next morning with a huge lump the size of a golf ball at the back of my heel. I'd ruptured my Achilles tendon and could hardly walk. It's strange how two small details like that can come together to dictate the shape of a poet's life for months, or years in this case. Before these two events, I had not thought much about Greek mythology. But when I started to read about the fate of Achilles, with his mortal father, immortal mother and bizarre extended family of gods, I was surprised and delighted to discover they all seemed so flawed and endearingly familiar: jealous, proud, nasty, charming, interfering, tender, horny, as well as vulnerable, vicious and easily vexed. In short, unmistakably human. At the very least, this small sequence should pique your curiosity enough to send you looking for translations of the great poet Homer for more of the story.

As for "*Le jardin du Vaucluse*," I have my friend and painter Wally Ballach in Provence to blame. He took me to visit his favourite spots in Avignon and Vaucluse. The famous Italian poet Petrarch is reported to have met or glimpsed Laura in a church in Avignon and would spend the next twenty-odd years trying immortalize his resulting emotions in poetry. For my part, I've tried to imagine Laura's take on this famously unconsummated, literary relationship.

"Northwest Passage" recounts some details of Ann's and my Yukon rafting trip from Margaret's Lake down the Firth River to the Beaufort Sea, thanks to an act of generosity from our friend Graham Porter. Mervin Joe was one of four Inuit Parks Canada employees who travelled with us taking water samples to see if the melting permafrost was releasing dangerous substances into the river. The details behind "David's Poem" were shared with me by Inuit David Hoagak, who was also working for Parks Canada during the same trip. He and Merv regaled us with stories during our evening sessions in a large round tent called The Marmot. They were both surprised and pleased to have contributed to the poems. "Sheep Slot Narrows" features several of the crew and Olivia Chow, former MP and widow of NDP leader Jack Layton. She was an unexpected but delightful and dynamic companion during that trip.

And, finally, "Royal Flush." I had the pleasure of meeting Mexican poet and activist Homero Aridjis and his wife Betty Ferber in Mexico City during my research for *Kingdom of Ten Thousand Things: An Impossible Journey from Kabul to Chiapas*, about the fifth-century Buddhist monk Huishen, who beat Columbus to the Americas by a thousand years. They are an amazingly engaged and creative couple. Homero's concern for the survival of monarch butterflies and other endangered species touched me deeply.

*Gary Geddes*
*Thetis Island*
*June, 2022*

# Acknowledgements

With every achievement, however modest, there are debts to be acknowledged, whether it's the parents who gave you birth, or those who raised you. And there are friends and loved ones who've put up with you and the solitudes you required to create, as well as the linguistic absorption, including puns, that often made you unbearable. So, my special gratitude goes out again to my stepmother Margaret Cosford, who was so gentle, forbearing and positive during the most difficult of times. So, too, the many friends who sacrificed precious hours to read and comment on my work, even in its most rudimentary stages. Thank you Ron Smith, Jim Anderson, Di Brandt, Art Joyce, Chris Knight, Bruce Rice, Andrew Mitchell, Mark Abley, the late John Asfour, my daughters Jenny, Bronwen and Charlotte, and my wife Ann Eriksson, whose heart must have sunk on more than one occasion when I showed up in her office dishevelled, hollow-eyed and clutching yet another ragged draft. Michael Mirolla at Guernica Editions did not hesitate when I first wrote to him about this manuscript and even, apparently, after he read it. For that and for his suggestions and unerring attention to detail, I am most grateful. To continue as a publisher during a pandemic, and at a time when the Internet has largely destroyed the conventional promotion and marketing of books, is an act of faith not to be minimized. I salute him and his untiring staff.

# About the Author

Gary Geddes has written and edited more than fifty books of poetry, fiction, drama, criticism, non-fiction, translation and anthologies, including *20th-Century Poetry and Poetics* (Oxford), and been the recipient of a dozen national and international literary awards, including the National Magazine Gold Award, the Commonwealth Poetry Prize (Americas Region), the Lt-Governor's Award for Literary Excellence, and the Gabriela Mistral Prize from the government of Chile, awarded simultaneously to Octavio Paz, Vaclav Havel, Ernesto Cardenal, Rafael Alberti and Mario Benedetti. His work has been translated into six languages and he has lectured and performed his work in twenty-one countries.

Before retiring, he taught English and Creative Writing at Concordia University and was the founder of Quadrant Editions and Cormorant Books. He has subsequently served as writer-in-residence at UBC, University of Ottawa, McMaster and the Vancouver Public Library, as well as visiting writer at the University of Missouri-St. Louis and Distinguished Professor of Canadian Culture at Western Washington University in Bellingham. He lives on Thetis Island with his wife, the novelist Ann Eriksson.

**Poetry:**

*Rivers Inlet*

*Snakeroot*

*Letter of the Master of Horse*

*War & other measures*

*The Acid Test*

*The Terracotta Army*

*Changes of State*

*Hong Kong*

*No Easy Exit / Salida difícil*

*Light of Burning Towers*

*Girl by the Water*

*The Perfect Cold Warrior*

*Active Trading: Selected Poems 1970–1995*

*Flying Blind*

*Skaldance*

*Falsework*

*Swimming Ginger*

*What Does A House Want?*

*The Resumption of Play*

*The Ventriloquist: Poetic Narratives from the Womb of War*

**Fiction:**

*The Unsettling of the West*

**Non-Fiction:**

*Letters from Managua: Meditations on Politics & Art*
*Sailing Home: A Journey through Time, Place & Memory*
*Kingdom of Ten Thousand Things: An Impossible Journey from Kabul to Chiapas*
*Drink the Bitter Root: A search for justice and healing in Africa*
*Medicine Unbundled: A Journey Through the Minefields of Indigenous Health Care*

**Drama:**

*Les Maudits Anglais* (1984)

**Criticism:**

*Conrad's Later Novels*
*Out of the Ordinary: Politics, Poetry & Narrative*
*Bearing Witness*

**Anthologies:**

*20th-Century Poetry & Poetics*
*Skookum Wawa: Writings of the Canadian Northwest*
*Chinada: Memoirs of the Gang of Seven*
*Vancouver: Soul of A City*
*Compañeros: Writings about Latin America*
*The Art of Short Fiction: An International Anthology*

MIX
Paper
FSC® C100212

Printed by Imprimerie Gauvin
Gatineau, Québec